KNOW THE WORLD OF
MIGHTY MACHINES

by Maureen Spurgeon

illustrated by Brian Bartle

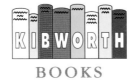

KIBWORTH

BOOKS

First published 1995
Reprinted 1997, 1999

Published by Kibworth Books
Imperial Road, Kibworth Beauchamp, Leicester LE8 0HR, England

Printed in Belgium

ISBN 0-7239-0076 0

CONTENTS

STEAM-DRIVEN MACHINES

The first people to have daily contact with steam-driven machines were factory workers in the fast-growing industrial towns of England around two hundred years ago. Apart from them, most other people had to wait until the introduction of public railways in 1875 before they even saw one. Then, gradually, machines powered by steam were put to work in other industries, such as farming.

STEAM-PLOUGH

When a steam-driven tractor was used to pull a plough, it was difficult to keep the towing line taut. Soon, two tractors, or one traction engine and one tractor, were being employed to pull the plough back and forth along a cable.

TRACTION ENGINE

A traction engine is an engine that draws or pulls a load. On the farm, it would tow the plough or the threshing-machine. It also provided the steam power. Connected to the enormous side wheel of the traction engine were belts which turned spindles on the machines to make them work. Here is a picture of the great Wantage Traction Engine, built in England in 1898.

STEAM-TRACTOR

Although the first steam-driven tractor was invented as early as 1770, it was not until more than one hundred years later that a farmer could actually buy one from a manufacturer. At that time, a tractor was twice the size of a modern car, and it had steel wheels with spikes round the rims to grip the soil.

THRESHING-MACHINE

A steam-driven thresher was the size of a house! At harvest time, farmers took it in turns to hire them, and some of these mighty machines were still in use only fifty years ago.

POUNDING, PUMPING, AND DIGGING

Before machines came into general use, all building, mining, and tunnelling work was done by manpower. Machines were able to do most of this work much more quickly and efficiently.

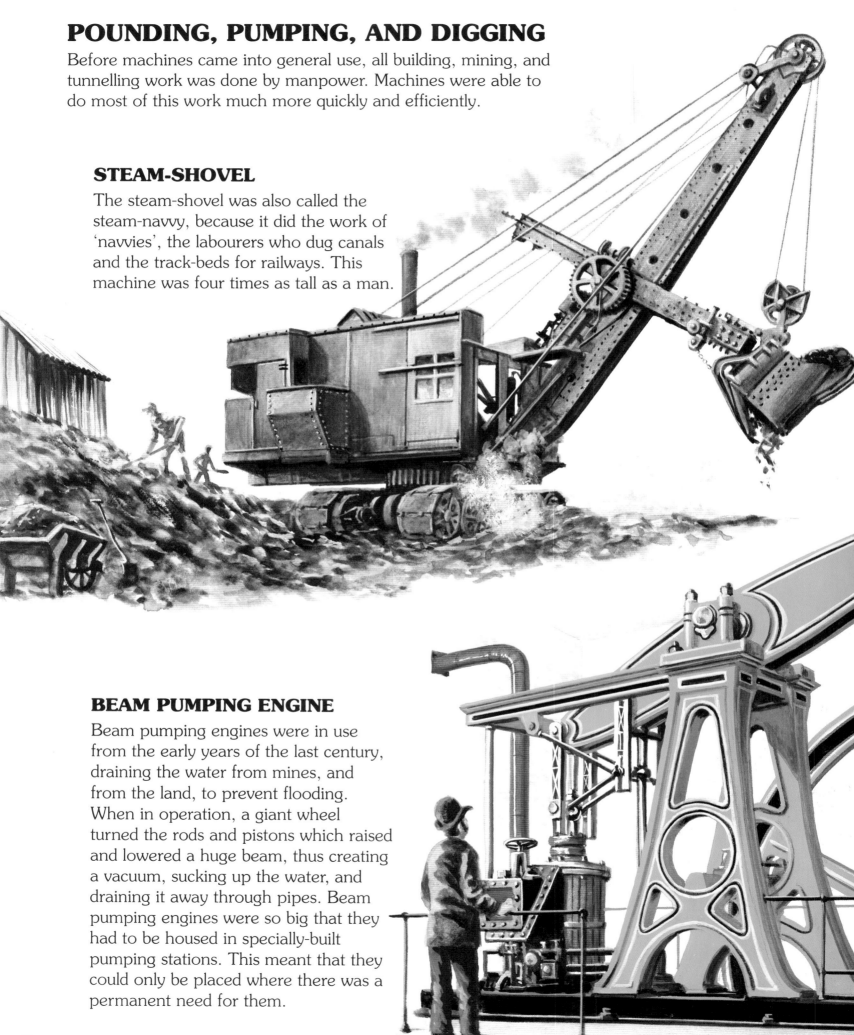

STEAM-SHOVEL

The steam-shovel was also called the steam-navvy, because it did the work of 'navvies', the labourers who dug canals and the track-beds for railways. This machine was four times as tall as a man.

BEAM PUMPING ENGINE

Beam pumping engines were in use from the early years of the last century, draining the water from mines, and from the land, to prevent flooding. When in operation, a giant wheel turned the rods and pistons which raised and lowered a huge beam, thus creating a vacuum, sucking up the water, and draining it away through pipes. Beam pumping engines were so big that they had to be housed in specially-built pumping stations. This meant that they could only be placed where there was a permanent need for them.

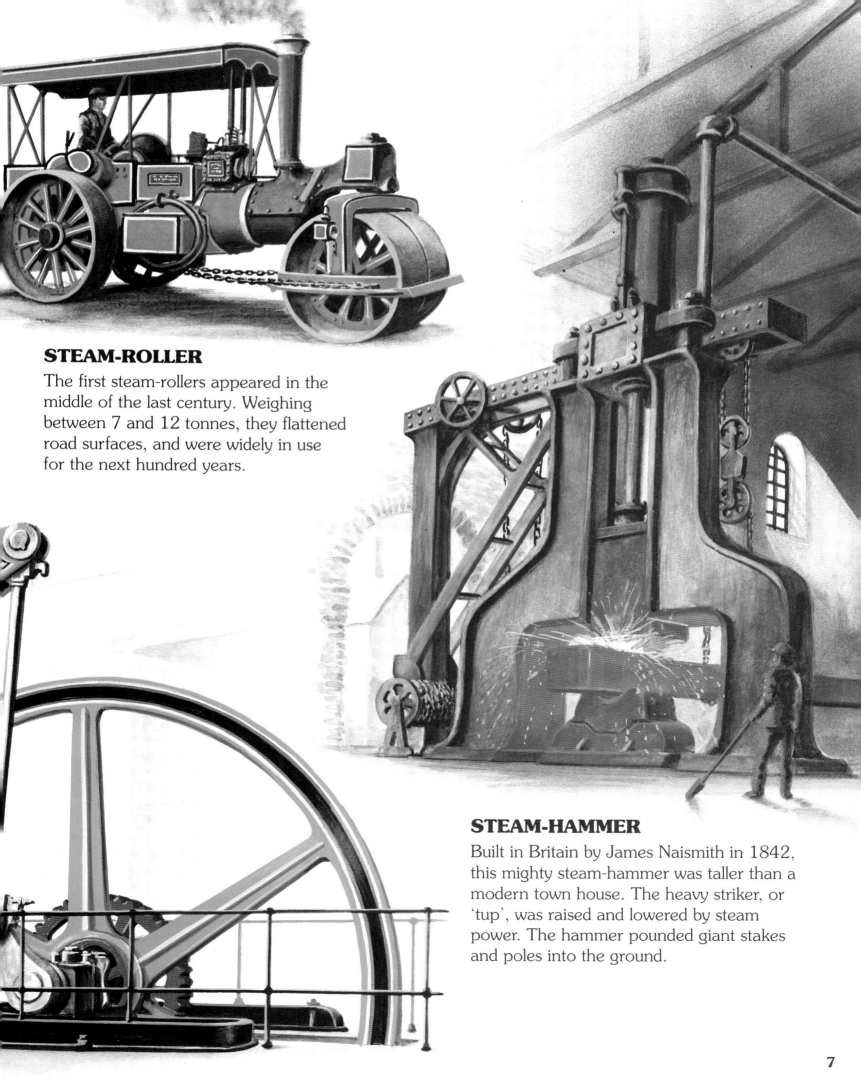

STEAM-ROLLER

The first steam-rollers appeared in the middle of the last century. Weighing between 7 and 12 tonnes, they flattened road surfaces, and were widely in use for the next hundred years.

STEAM-HAMMER

Built in Britain by James Naismith in 1842, this mighty steam-hammer was taller than a modern town house. The heavy striker, or 'tup', was raised and lowered by steam power. The hammer pounded giant stakes and poles into the ground.

TRACTORS AND TOOLS

Although farmers understood how much time a tractor could save them, and what work it could do for them, for a very long time, even after manufacturers started making them, a tractor was too expensive for a farmer to purchase. Horses remained the most common form of power on a farm up until the late 1930s. By then, a whole range of new tools had been developed for use with a tractor, so that it was able to do even more work for its owner.

PLOUGH

At first, tractor-pulled ploughs could only dig one or two furrows at a time. Now, six or more furrows can be ploughed simultaneously.

POST-DRIVER

With a post-driver fixed to the back of his tractor, a farmer can put a fence around a large field in a single day. The post-driver's heavy striker slides up and down, banging the posts into the ground.

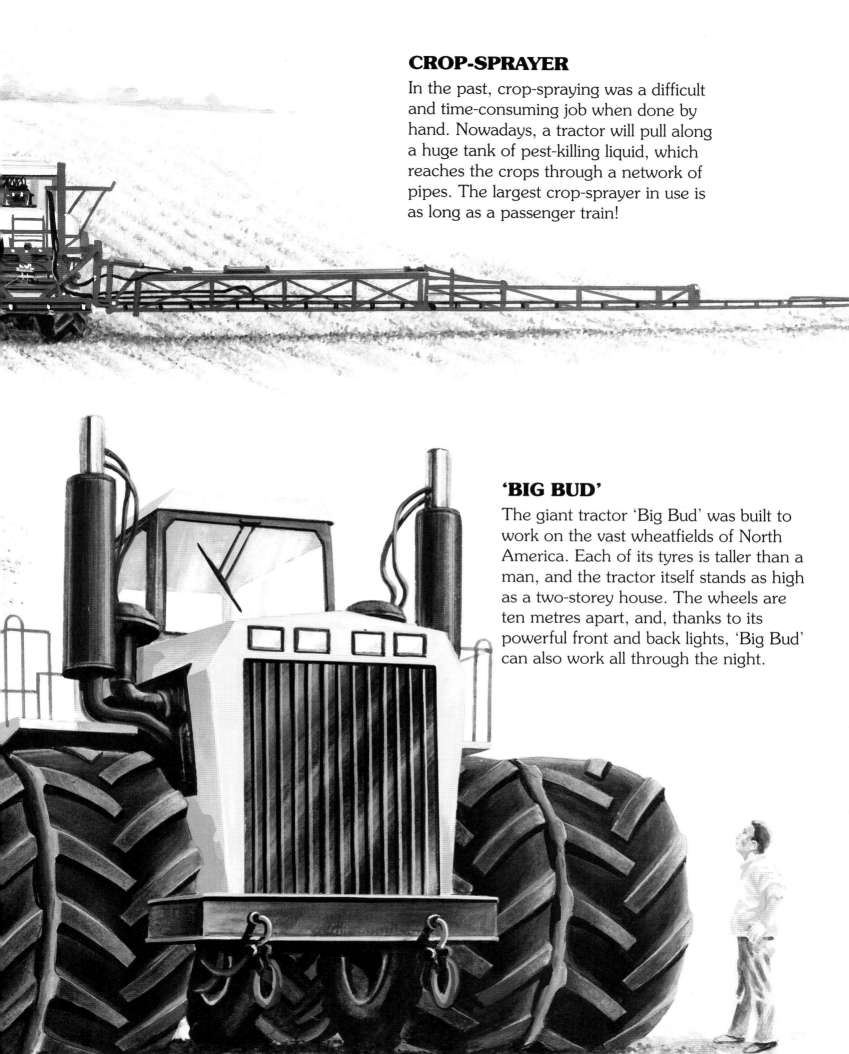

CROP-SPRAYER

In the past, crop-spraying was a difficult and time-consuming job when done by hand. Nowadays, a tractor will pull along a huge tank of pest-killing liquid, which reaches the crops through a network of pipes. The largest crop-sprayer in use is as long as a passenger train!

'BIG BUD'

The giant tractor 'Big Bud' was built to work on the vast wheatfields of North America. Each of its tyres is taller than a man, and the tractor itself stands as high as a two-storey house. The wheels are ten metres apart, and, thanks to its powerful front and back lights, 'Big Bud' can also work all through the night.

HARVESTING BY MACHINE

The harvest is the end-result of a whole year's hard work by the farmer . . . and everything can be spoiled by even a short spell of bad weather at harvest-time. Speed is essential when the crops are being brought in. Through the use of machinery, the work of harvesting can be done in much less time than when the job had to be done by human labour alone.

BIG-BALER

When the combine harvester has cut down the crop, the big-baler gathers up the straw that remains, and rolls it, or bundles it, into huge bales. Each bale weighs as much as eight men.

ROOT-CROP HARVESTER

Root-crops, such as potatoes, carrots, onions, or turnips, are dug up by the root-crop harvester. The machine then strips off the leaves, takes the vegetables up a small elevator, and tips them on to a moving belt. There is room on the machine for a team of pickers to stand beside this belt, taking out any bad or damaged produce, before the rest of the crop goes into a separate trailer.

COMBINE HARVESTER

The first combine harvesters were drawn by tractors. Now, a combine harvester is a machine in its own right. After it has cut and then threshed the crop, the grain is poured out into a lorry or other container. Giant combine harvesters can produce up to 15 tonnes of grain per hour.

MILLS AND WHEELS

Only a few of the largest machines made in the world today can equal the size of the mills and wheels powered by wind or water.

WINDMILLS

For many hundreds of years, windmills have been used for grinding corn into flour. A sail on one of these windmills had a length similar to that of a modern container lorry. These sails turned a 10-metre diameter wheel inside the mill, and that wheel turned a huge spindle.

WATER-WHEEL

The largest water-wheels built were nearly 28m in diameter . . . that's more than twice the width of a tennis court! A series of buckets, each one capable of holding two men, were fixed to the rim of the wheel. As water from a long overhead channel filled each bucket in turn, its weight caused the wheel to rotate.

WIND FARMS

A wind farm is the name given to an area of land, a 'farm', on which from 15 to 20 giant windmills are built, for the purpose of generating electricity. The tower of one of the smallest of these windmills could be 25m high, and it would have a propeller-type sail measuring up to 30m from tip to tip. A windmill of this kind can generate enough electricity for the needs of about 250 houses.

EXCAVATORS AND EARTH-MOVERS

Excavators and earth-movers are machines which dig and move earth. Some of these machines are used for digging the foundations of buildings or roads, and others dig deep trenches and tunnels.

BACKHOE LOADER

This machine has a bucket at the back, and a loader, or loading shovel, at the front. The largest of these machines is twice the height of a man, and as long as a football pitch!

BACKHOE EXCAVATOR

The vast metal bucket of a backhoe excavator can dig out up to 1.5 tonnes of earth at a time . . . more than the combined weight of 18 men!

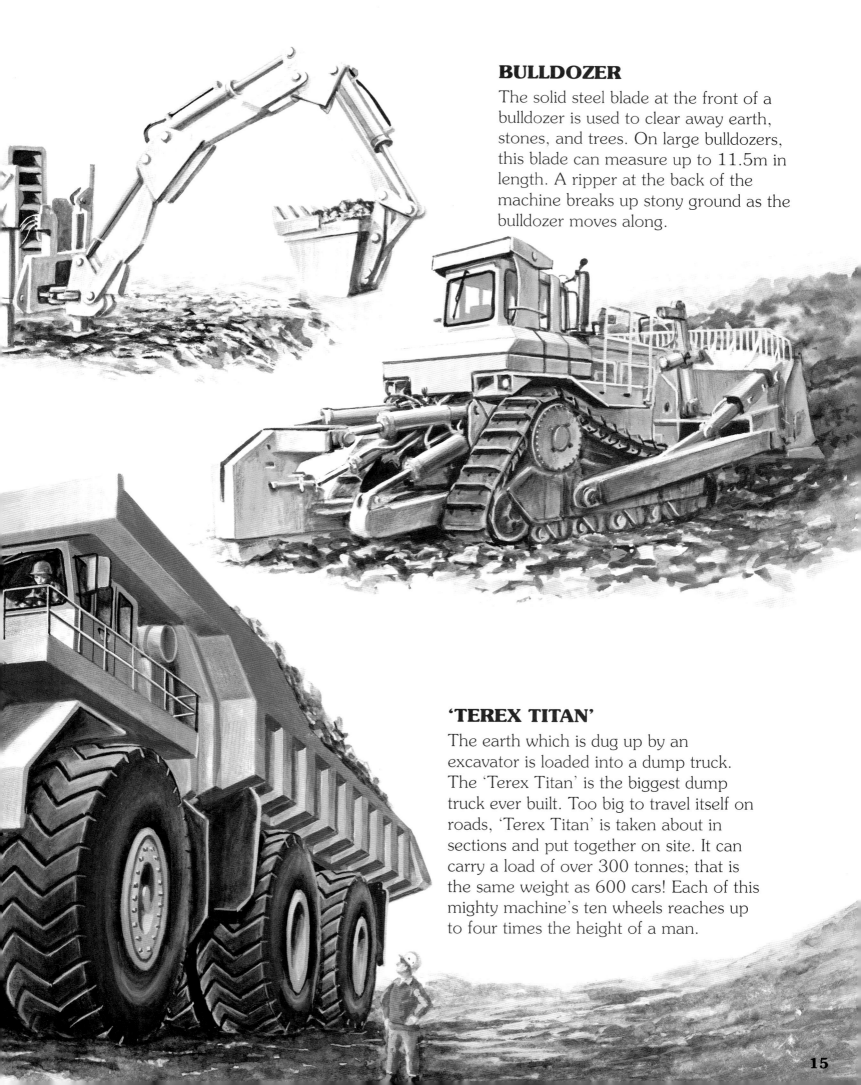

BULLDOZER

The solid steel blade at the front of a bulldozer is used to clear away earth, stones, and trees. On large bulldozers, this blade can measure up to 11.5m in length. A ripper at the back of the machine breaks up stony ground as the bulldozer moves along.

'TEREX TITAN'

The earth which is dug up by an excavator is loaded into a dump truck. The 'Terex Titan' is the biggest dump truck ever built. Too big to travel itself on roads, 'Terex Titan' is taken about in sections and put together on site. It can carry a load of over 300 tonnes; that is the same weight as 600 cars! Each of this mighty machine's ten wheels reaches up to four times the height of a man.

MOBILE CRANES

All cranes are used to move and lift heavy loads. There are many different types of crane, each doing a different type of work. Mobile cranes are those which can be driven from place to place, to wherever they are needed.

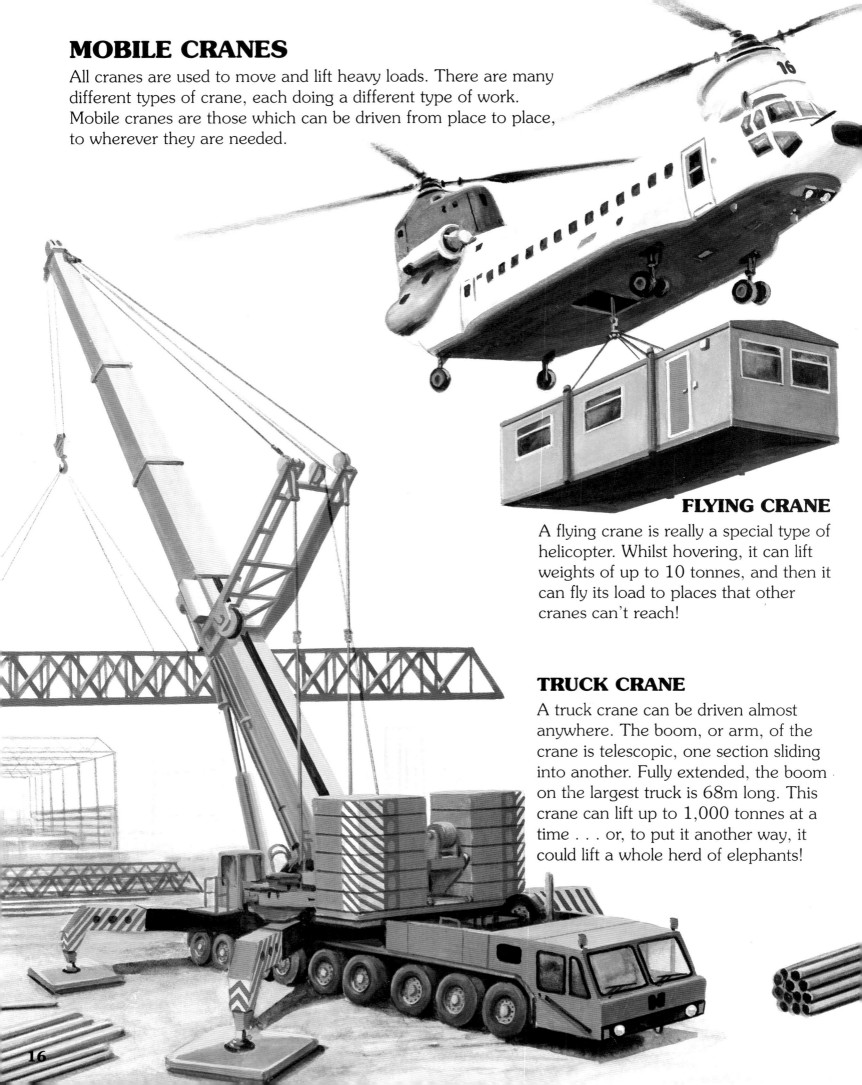

FLYING CRANE

A flying crane is really a special type of helicopter. Whilst hovering, it can lift weights of up to 10 tonnes, and then it can fly its load to places that other cranes can't reach!

TRUCK CRANE

A truck crane can be driven almost anywhere. The boom, or arm, of the crane is telescopic, one section sliding into another. Fully extended, the boom on the largest truck is 68m long. This crane can lift up to 1,000 tonnes at a time . . . or, to put it another way, it could lift a whole herd of elephants!

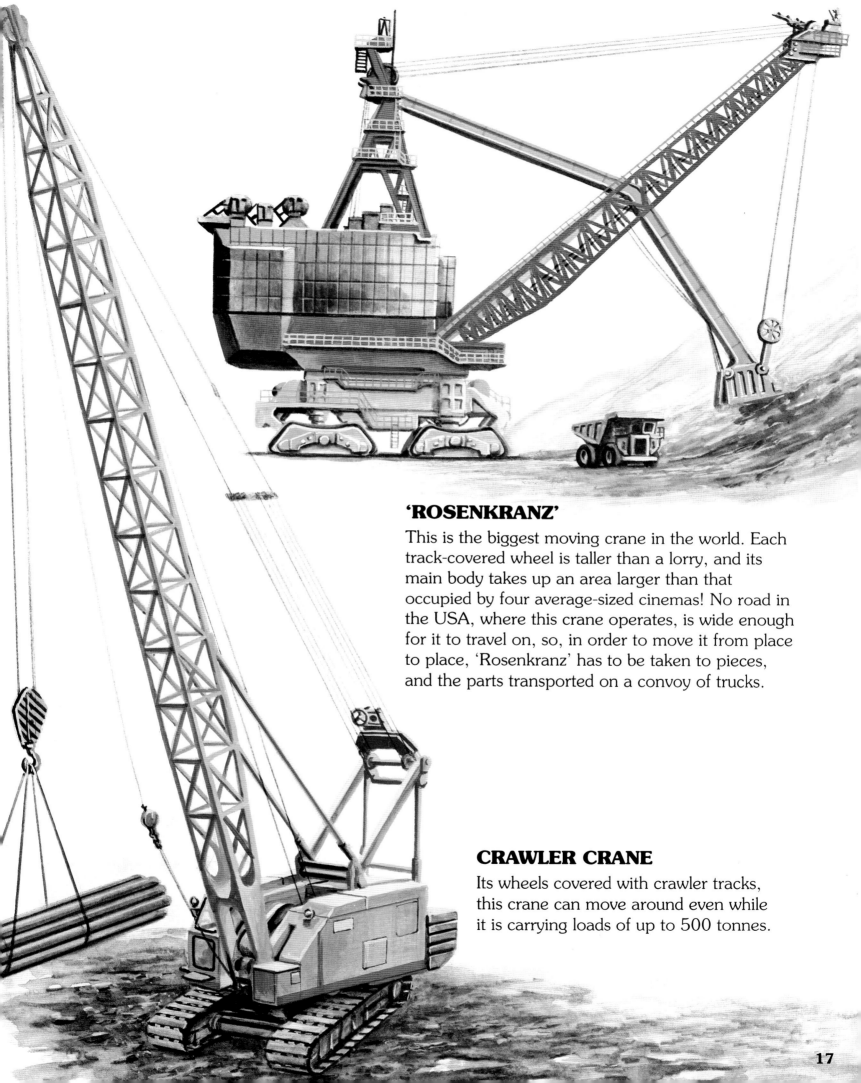

'ROSENKRANZ'

This is the biggest moving crane in the world. Each track-covered wheel is taller than a lorry, and its main body takes up an area larger than that occupied by four average-sized cinemas! No road in the USA, where this crane operates, is wide enough for it to travel on, so, in order to move it from place to place, 'Rosenkranz' has to be taken to pieces, and the parts transported on a convoy of trucks.

CRAWLER CRANE

Its wheels covered with crawler tracks, this crane can move around even while it is carrying loads of up to 500 tonnes.

TRAVELLING CRANES

Travelling cranes have wheels, and they 'travel' along tracks or rails, taking loads from one place to another. The rails along which they move can be on the ground or overhead, outdoors or in.

CONTAINER CRANE

Container cranes are mostly seen on the quaysides in harbours, loading and unloading containers on and off ships. The average height of one of these cranes is 60m, and their length 80m.

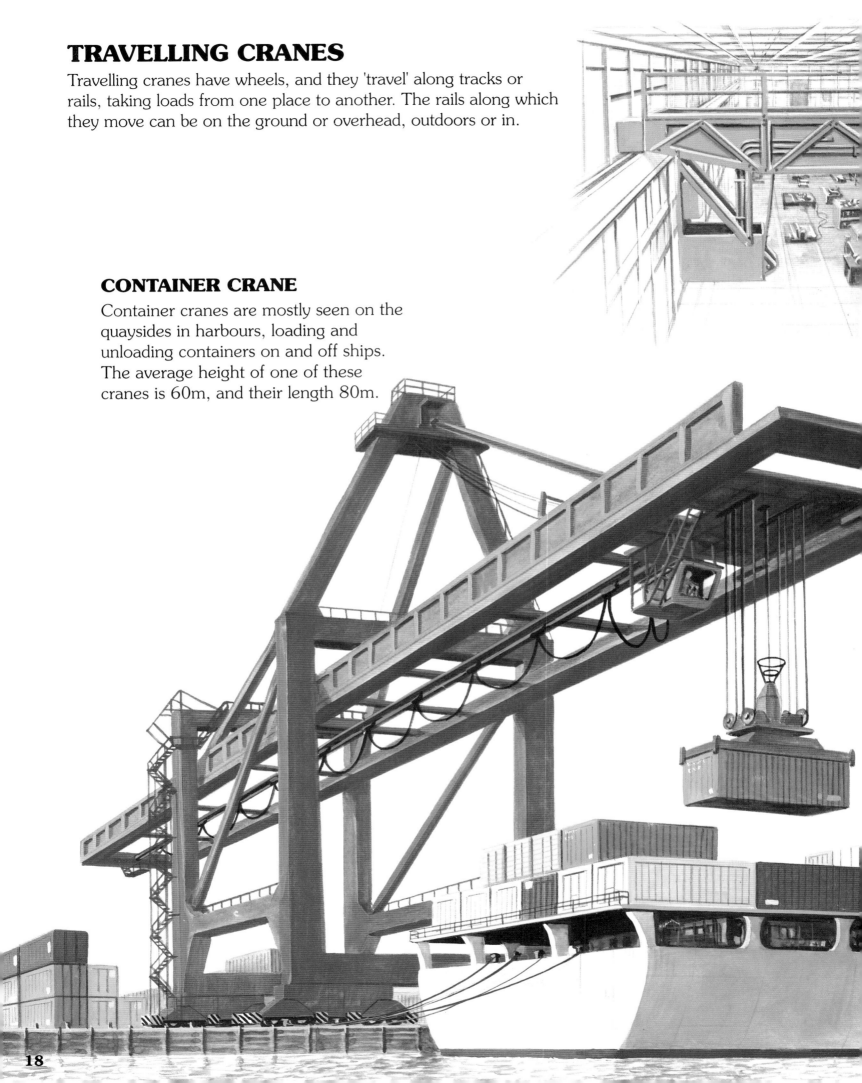

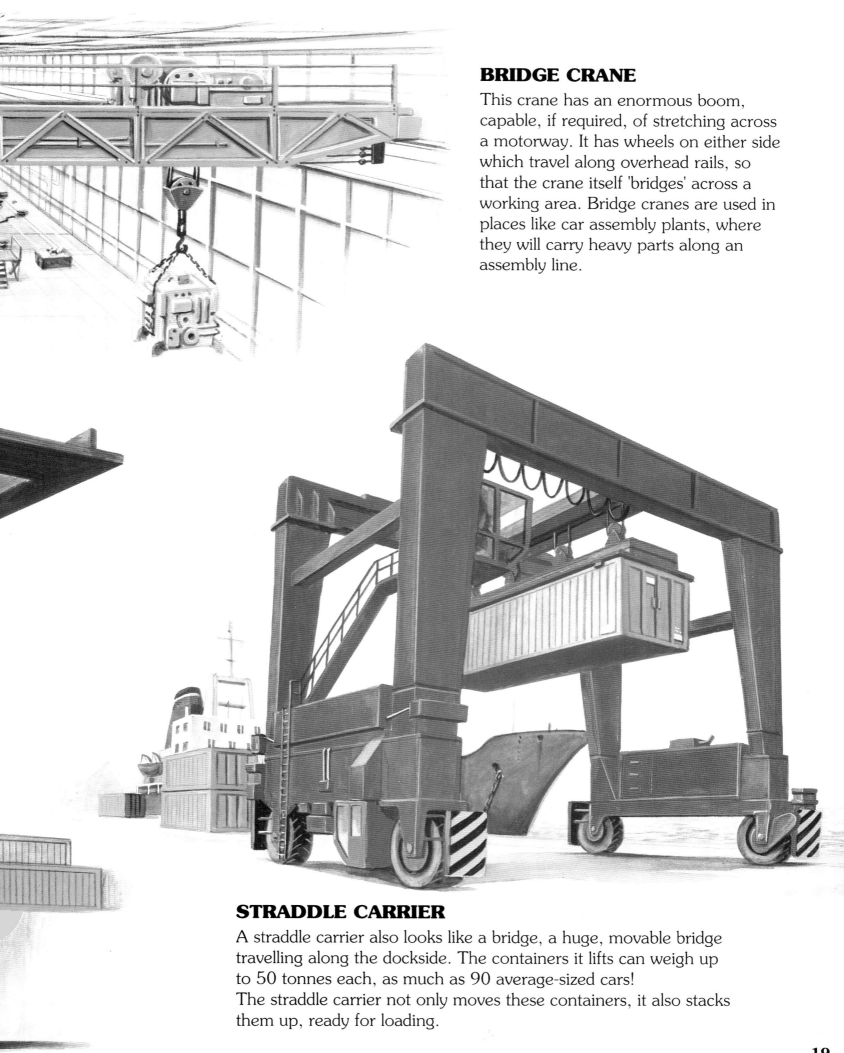

BRIDGE CRANE

This crane has an enormous boom, capable, if required, of stretching across a motorway. It has wheels on either side which travel along overhead rails, so that the crane itself 'bridges' across a working area. Bridge cranes are used in places like car assembly plants, where they will carry heavy parts along an assembly line.

STRADDLE CARRIER

A straddle carrier also looks like a bridge, a huge, movable bridge travelling along the dockside. The containers it lifts can weigh up to 50 tonnes each, as much as 90 average-sized cars!
The straddle carrier not only moves these containers, it also stacks them up, ready for loading.

19

DEMOLITION

It is hard work knocking down buildings. So the tools used for demolition must be especially powerful and tough. Usually, these tools are attached to an excavator or a crane.

DROP-BALL DEMOLISHER

A drop-ball is attached by two cables to a crawler crane. Made of lead or solid steel, the drop-ball will weigh at least 5 tonnes, twice as much as a hippopotamus!

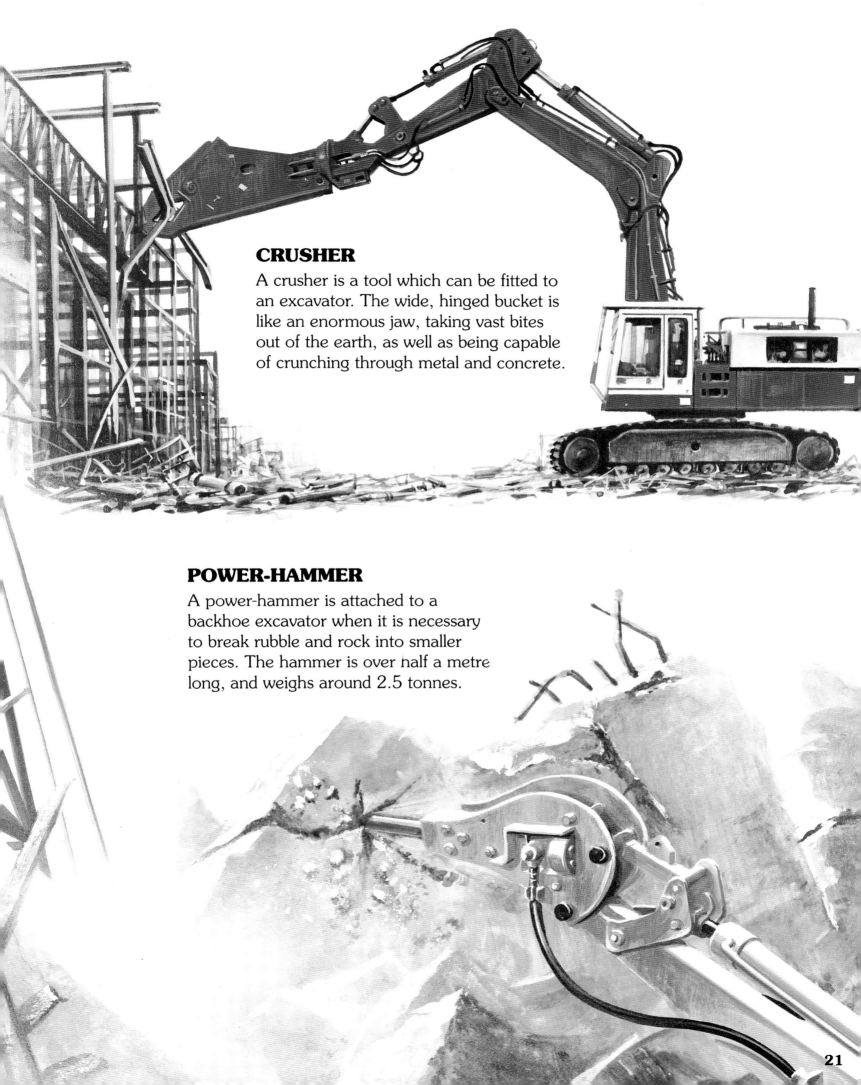

CRUSHER

A crusher is a tool which can be fitted to an excavator. The wide, hinged bucket is like an enormous jaw, taking vast bites out of the earth, as well as being capable of crunching through metal and concrete.

POWER-HAMMER

A power-hammer is attached to a backhoe excavator when it is necessary to break rubble and rock into smaller pieces. The hammer is over half a metre long, and weighs around 2.5 tonnes.

MACHINES FOR BUILDING WORK

As the average height of buildings in large towns becomes greater, so the machines used in constructing them have to be larger and stronger. Some of the biggest of these machines are used in the building of high-rise apartments and office blocks.

TOWER CRANE

A tower crane arrives at a building site in sections. As the new building grows in height, additional sections are added to the tower crane, and bolted on. The tower crane's boom can be almost as long as a soccer pitch.

CONCRETE MIXER

The stone, sand, and cement which make up concrete are mixed in the drum as the concrete mixer is being driven to the building site. The drum is so large that you could fit a car inside it.

CONCRETE PUMP

This machine sucks up concrete from a big tank or hopper at the back, then pumps it out through a pipe that is 25m long . . . more than the length of three buses.

DROP-HAMMER CRANE

The task of the drop-hammer crane is to drive steel piles into the ground when the foundations of buildings are being laid. The hammer, which weighs up to 8 tonnes, is dropped from a height of up to 80cm.

AUGER CRANE

'Auger' is the name for a large screw or drill, and the auger crane is often called the 'drilling crane.' The auger, which is fixed to the top of the crane's boom, is as tall as a high-rise block of flats.

CRANES AT SEA

Huge floating cranes load and unload ships when there are no travelling cranes available to do the work. Other sea-going cranes are used for building deep-sea oil or gas rigs. These cranes are among the largest that have been made.

FLOATING CRANE

A floating crane is built on a pontoon, or floating platform. Heavy ropes link the pontoon to the edge of the quay until the loading or unloading of a cargo ship has been completed. The largest of these floating cranes can be three times as high as a house.

SEMI-SUBMERSIBLE CRANE VESSEL

'Semi-submersible' means partly underwater. This giant machine sails from one job to another. It has a crawler crane which moves around its 154m-long deck, as well as two enormous cranes that work together to lift whole sections of oil rigs and gas platforms into position. Each crane can lift up to 1,000 tonnes . . . as much as the weight of a ship! Over 300 men live and work on the crane vessel for months at a time.

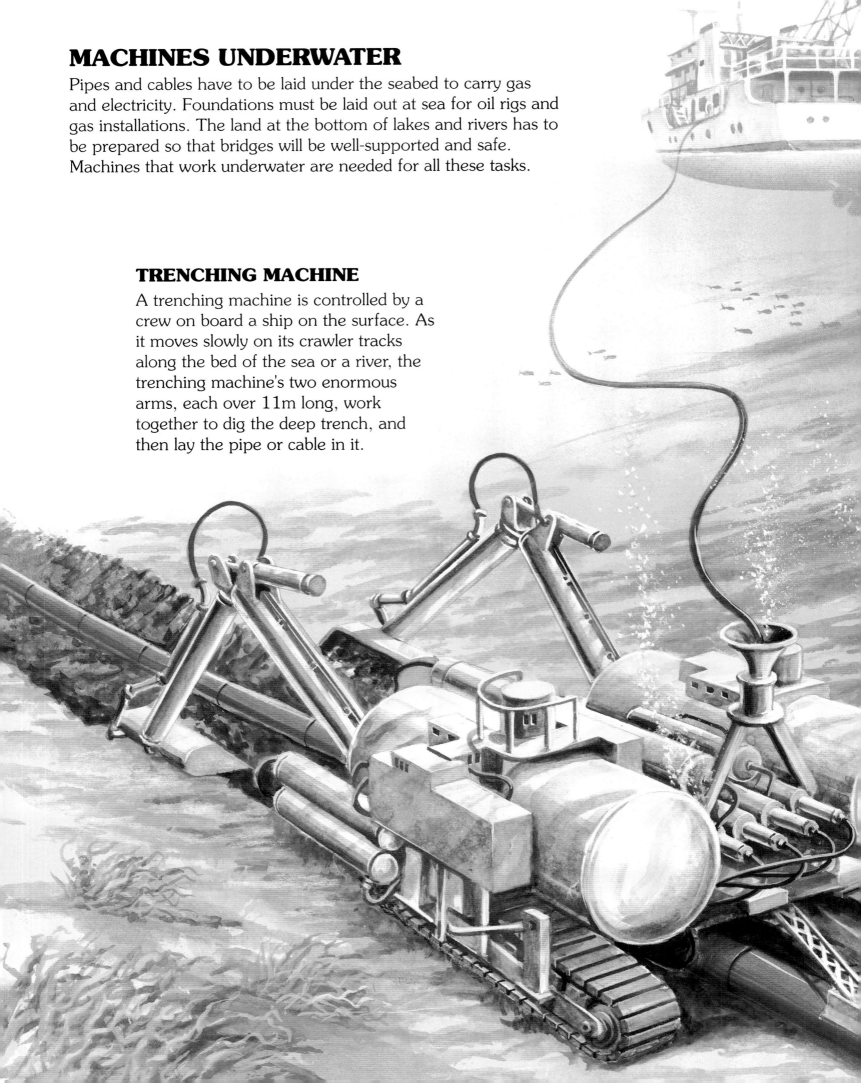

MACHINES UNDERWATER

Pipes and cables have to be laid under the seabed to carry gas and electricity. Foundations must be laid out at sea for oil rigs and gas installations. The land at the bottom of lakes and rivers has to be prepared so that bridges will be well-supported and safe. Machines that work underwater are needed for all these tasks.

TRENCHING MACHINE

A trenching machine is controlled by a crew on board a ship on the surface. As it moves slowly on its crawler tracks along the bed of the sea or a river, the trenching machine's two enormous arms, each over 11m long, work together to dig the deep trench, and then lay the pipe or cable in it.

UNDERWATER BULLDOZER

Before a bridge can be built, an underwater bulldozer is lowered from a ship to the bottom of the sea or a river to clear an area of ground, just as an ordinary building site is cleared on the land. The underwater bulldozer works at depths of up to 60m. It weighs around 20 tonnes.

DREDGERS

To avoid the risk of ships running aground where the water is shallow, sand or mud is removed from the bottom of seas, rivers, and canals, by a special machine called a dredger. After it is taken up into the dredger, this sand or mud is then either dumped elsewhere out at sea, or loaded into a waiting barge and carried away.

BUCKET DREDGER

A bucket dredger has a chain of buckets, called a 'ladder', mounted on a special frame. Each bucket, as it scoops up sand and mud from the seabed, is carried up this ladder, then the contents are tipped down a chute into a barge. Even the smallest bucket dredger is twice the size of an average house.

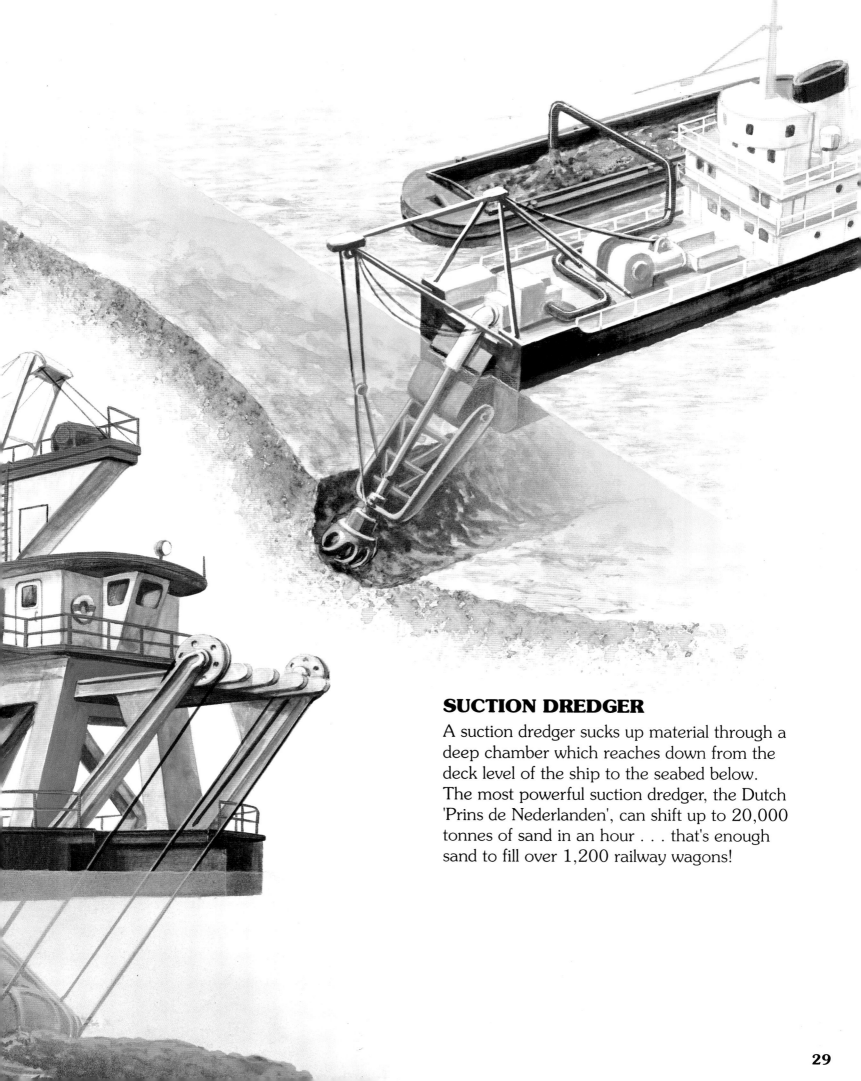

SUCTION DREDGER

A suction dredger sucks up material through a deep chamber which reaches down from the deck level of the ship to the seabed below. The most powerful suction dredger, the Dutch 'Prins de Nederlanden', can shift up to 20,000 tonnes of sand in an hour . . . that's enough sand to fill over 1,200 railway wagons!

ROAD-BUILDING MACHINES

Ancient civilisations built roads with layers of gravel, sand, and stone. Our modern roads are built in much the same way, except that, on top, there are layers of hot tarmac, or asphalt, which consists of hot tar and small stones mixed together.

GRADER

A grader has a heavy steel blade which smooths a bottom layer of stones over the ground. Its blade is over 4m long.

SCRAPER

A scraper is over 7m long. It levels the ground, cutting down all the lumps and bumps with sharp metal plates mounted on a belt which moves round as the machine goes along. The earth that is scraped loose is then gathered in a big metal box.

ROAD-ROLLER

This machine does the same work as the steam-roller in the past. Nowadays, the roller wheels are hollow steel, filled with sand or water, making them even heavier than the solid steel wheels of the old steam-roller.

PAVER

At the front of the paver is a large container called a hopper, which is filled with asphalt. As the paver goes along, the asphalt comes out at the back of the machine, where a thick steel blade spreads it out evenly.

MACHINES FOR MINING

An open-cast mine, where coal can be mined at ground level, has to cover a large area in order to give the same yield as an underground mine. So the machinery used in this form of mining is also on a vast scale. These giant machines remove the layers of earth on top, and then bring the coal to the surface from depths of up to 50m.

BUCKET-WHEEL EXCAVATOR

A bucket-wheel excavator has up to 18 great buckets fitted to an enormous wheel which revolves at the end of a long boom. A bucket can scoop up more than a tonne of coal at a time. If you can imagine ten buses laid end to end, you will have some idea of the diameter of the excavator's huge wheel!

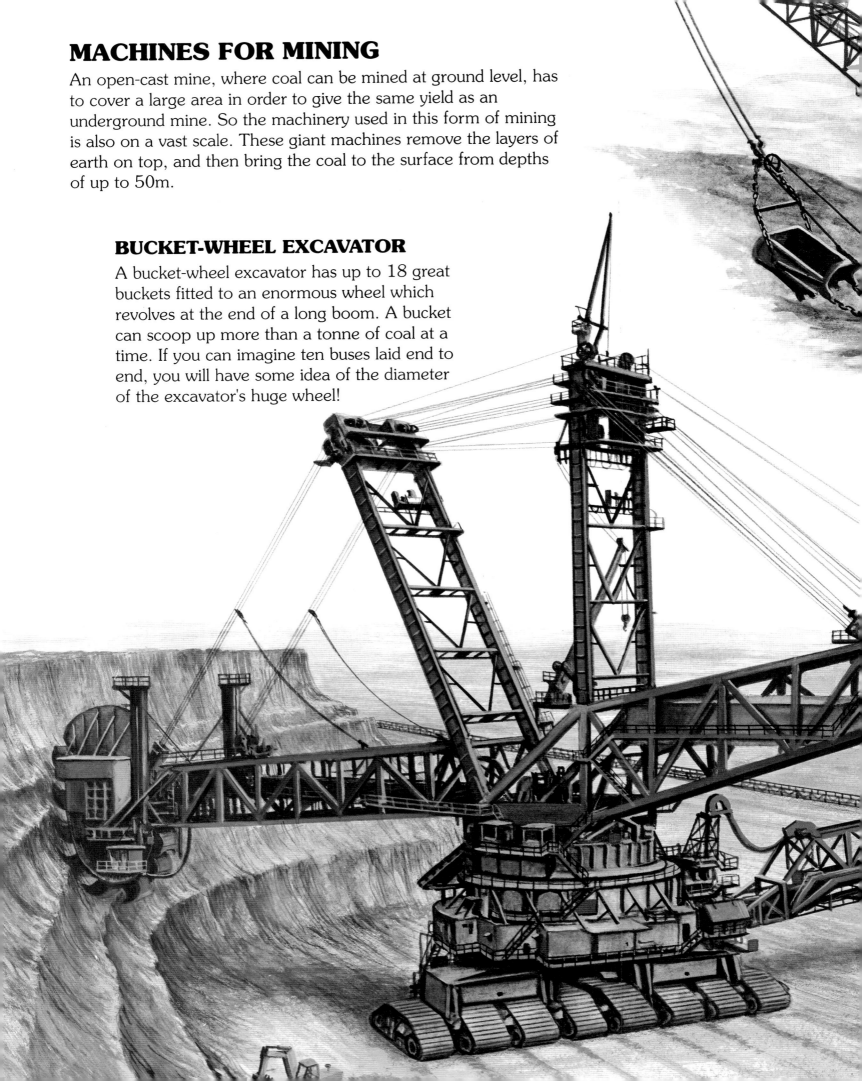

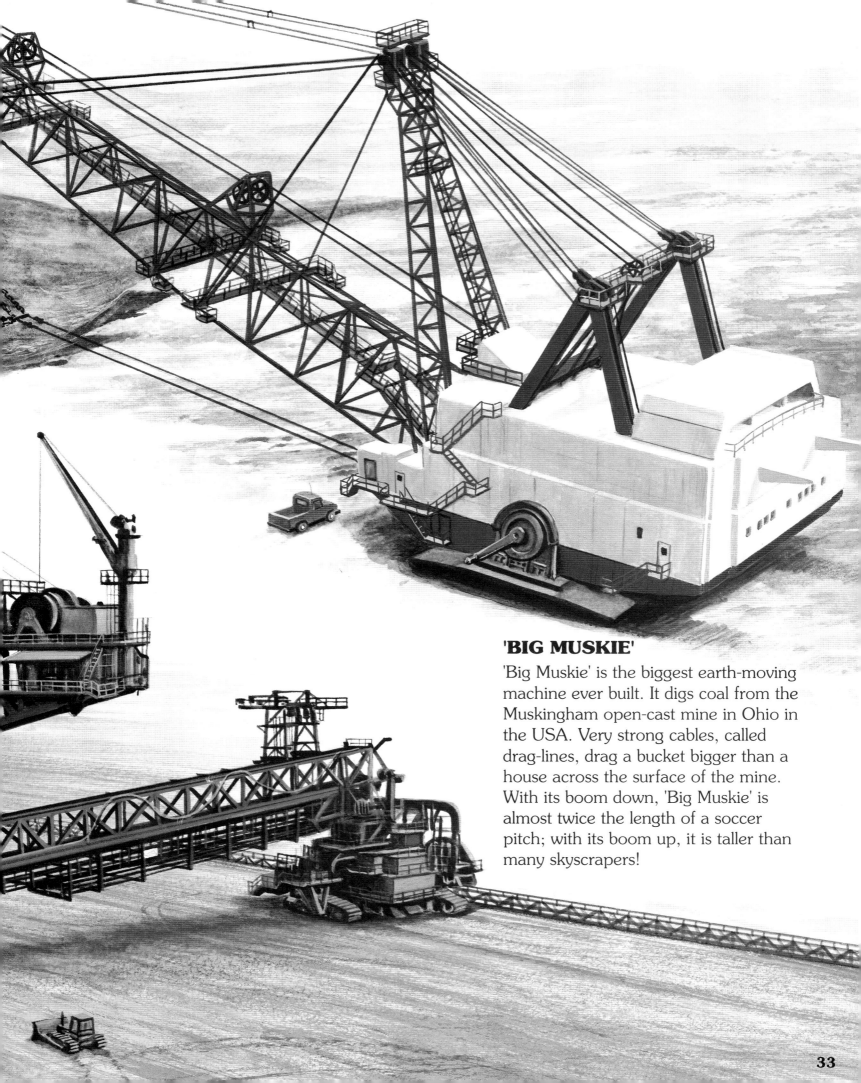

'BIG MUSKIE'

'Big Muskie' is the biggest earth-moving machine ever built. It digs coal from the Muskingham open-cast mine in Ohio in the USA. Very strong cables, called drag-lines, drag a bucket bigger than a house across the surface of the mine. With its boom down, 'Big Muskie' is almost twice the length of a soccer pitch; with its boom up, it is taller than many skyscrapers!

UNDERGROUND GIANTS

Until little more than 120 years ago, all underground mining was done by men using picks and shovels. It was manpower and explosives that bored the road and railway tunnels out of the earth. Then machines began to be used.

ROAD-HEADER

Small tunnels called 'headings' are dug by the road-header. This machine has a cup-shaped head, covered with steel blades, which spins round to cut through solid rock. A road header weighs 42 tonnes, or to put it another way, five times the weight of a big fire engine! It is also 10m high, and 9m long.

TUNNEL-BORING MACHINES

At around 270m long, tunnel-boring machines, or TBMs, are the biggest tunnelling machines in the world. As the head of the machine bores its way forward, concrete sections are carried along a conveyor belt to an erector which lines the inside of the tunnel with them. A TBM can dig through over 6m of earth in an hour, cutting a tunnel which can be up to 10m in diameter.

CONTINUOUS MINER

A continuous miner uses sharp blades called 'picks' to cut coal from the walls of a mine. The picks are mounted on a track driven by a wheel at the head of the machine, which is over 10.5m long.

MACHINES FOR SPECIAL JOBS

Some of the most unusual and strange-looking of the mighty machines are those which have been designed and built to do a specific job of work.

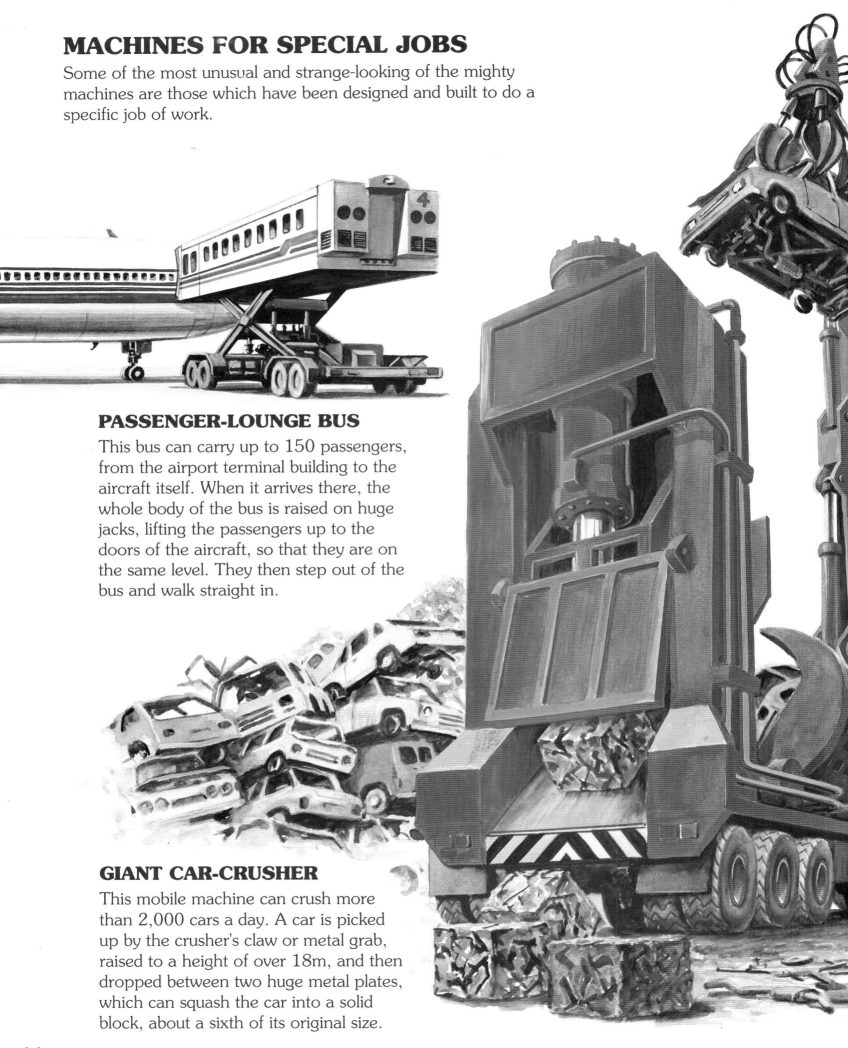

PASSENGER-LOUNGE BUS

This bus can carry up to 150 passengers, from the airport terminal building to the aircraft itself. When it arrives there, the whole body of the bus is raised on huge jacks, lifting the passengers up to the doors of the aircraft, so that they are on the same level. They then step out of the bus and walk straight in.

GIANT CAR-CRUSHER

This mobile machine can crush more than 2,000 cars a day. A car is picked up by the crusher's claw or metal grab, raised to a height of over 18m, and then dropped between two huge metal plates, which can squash the car into a solid block, about a sixth of its original size.

FIRE ENGINE

The largest fire engine today weighs over 30 tonnes. With its boom and escape platform capable of extending to heights of over 32m, firemen can use the fire engine to rescue people from high-rise apartment buildings and office blocks.

MACHINES ON THE MOVE

When large loads have to be moved from place to place, huge machines are sometimes needed to transport them. And the bigger the load, the stronger the machine has to be.

THE CRAWLER

This gigantic transporter has the task of carrying the American Space Shuttle to its launch pad at Cape Canaveral in Florida. The crawler is a huge, moving platform mounted on eight sets of caterpillar tracks, each track more than twice the height of a man. The vast machine itself is over 32m long, over 26m wide, and over 16.5m high. The combined weight of the rocket and the crawler is over 8,000 tonnes. Because of its size, the crawler can move at no more than 1.6km/h.

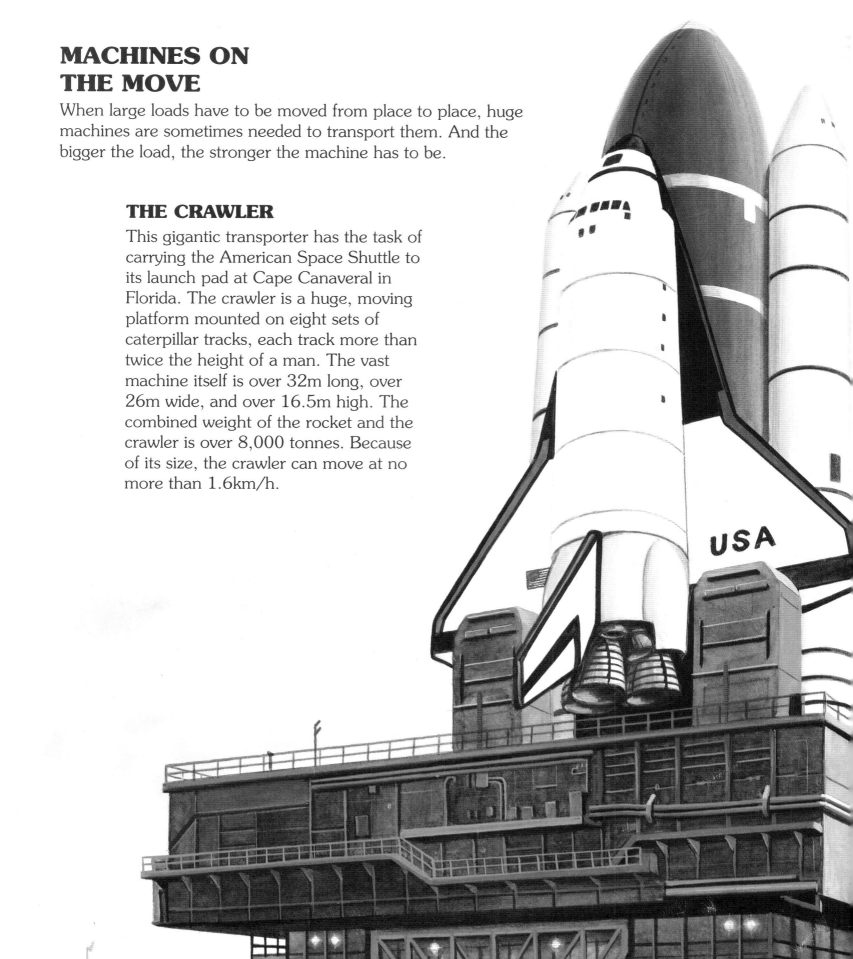

ROAD-TRAIN

The biggest trucks in the world are those which pull the road-trains in Australia and North America. Three or four huge trailers are linked together to make up a train, which is pulled along by a powerful driving unit. Road-trains travel thousands of kilometres, taking goods and supplies to isolated places.

GIANTS OF THE AIR

The quickest form of transportation is by air, both for passengers and cargo. With more and more people wanting to reach far-distant destinations speedily, and more and more supplies having to be delivered urgently to faraway parts of the world in emergency situations, ever bigger and more powerful aircraft have had to be constructed to meet these demands.

JUMBO JET – THE BOEING 747

This jet is the world's largest passenger airliner, capable of seating over 650 people on its two decks. It has a wingspan of nearly 60m, and it is over 70m in length; so it sits on an area about three times the size of a tennis court!

CONCORDE

Concorde is the world's first supersonic airliner, built to fly at more than twice the speed of sound; that's over 2,300 km/h! Concorde has a wingspan of nearly 29m, and it has been in passenger service since 1976.

THE US LOCKHEED C-58 GALAXY

This mighty aircraft can carry up to 370 troops, and, when its large, hinged nose is raised, 14 tanks can be driven into the massive cargo bay, which is over 40m long, and 6m wide. The Galaxy has a wingspan of over 67m, which is wider than a soccer pitch. On the runway, the aircraft rests on 28 enormous wheels.

THE WORLD'S LARGEST HELICOPTER

The Russian-built 'Mil-12 Homer' weighs over 100 tonnes, and is able to lift nearly 40 tonnes in weight at a time. It has a span of no less than 67m across its rotor tips.

MIGHTY MACHINES OF THE SEA

The biggest vessels on the sea are among the largest machines man has ever made.

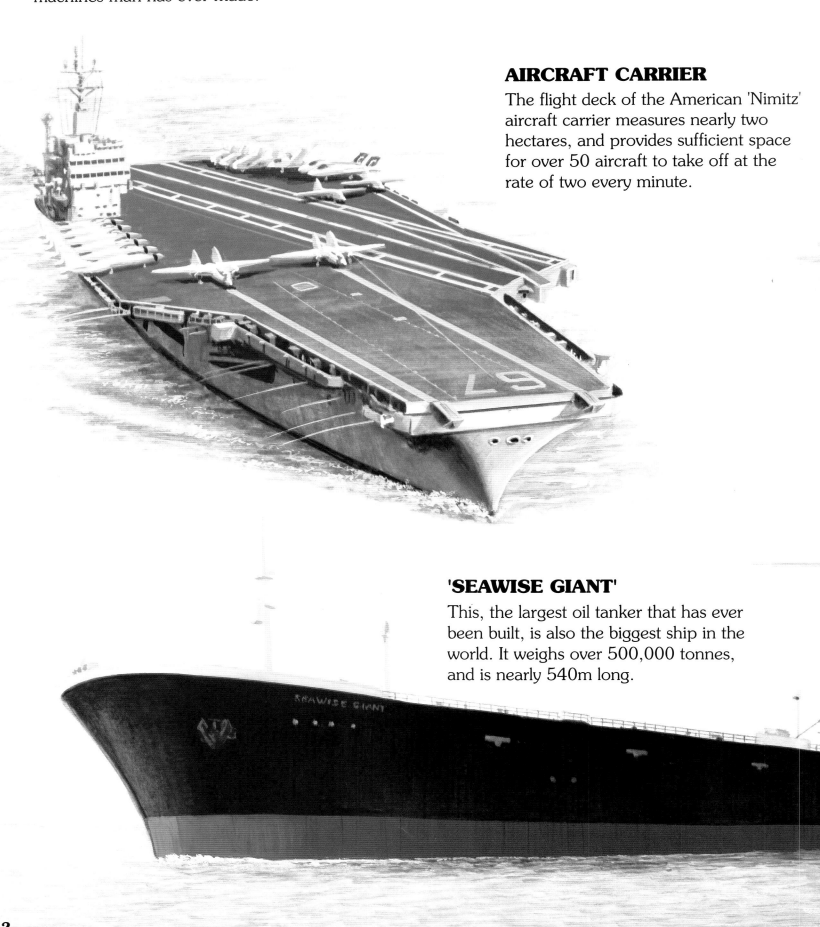

AIRCRAFT CARRIER

The flight deck of the American 'Nimitz' aircraft carrier measures nearly two hectares, and provides sufficient space for over 50 aircraft to take off at the rate of two every minute.

'SEAWISE GIANT'

This, the largest oil tanker that has ever been built, is also the biggest ship in the world. It weighs over 500,000 tonnes, and is nearly 540m long.

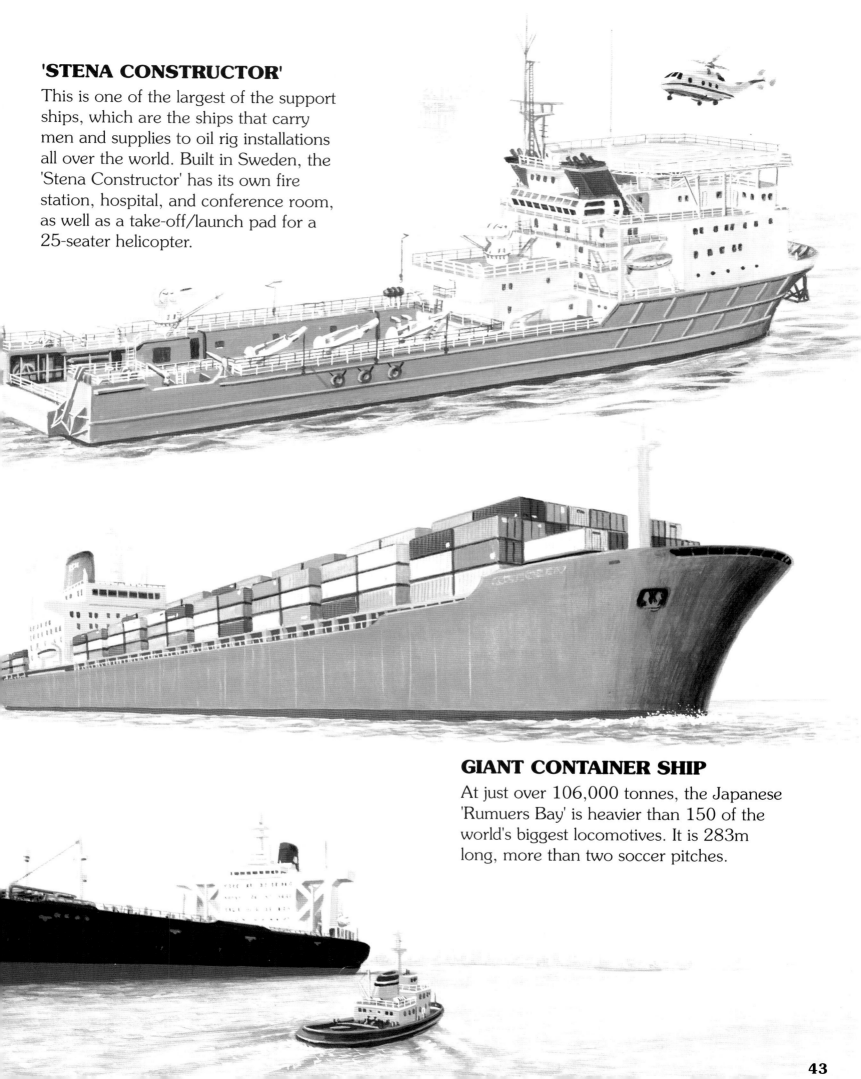

'STENA CONSTRUCTOR'

This is one of the largest of the support ships, which are the ships that carry men and supplies to oil rig installations all over the world. Built in Sweden, the 'Stena Constructor' has its own fire station, hospital, and conference room, as well as a take-off/launch pad for a 25-seater helicopter.

GIANT CONTAINER SHIP

At just over 106,000 tonnes, the Japanese 'Rumuers Bay' is heavier than 150 of the world's biggest locomotives. It is 283m long, more than two soccer pitches.

GIANT LOCOMOTIVES

The first locomotives were steam-driven. Then came the diesel-powered locomotives, and finally today's modern electric locomotives. No matter what the type of locomotive, the main requirement has always been that they should have the strength and power to haul heavy trains over long distances.

'BIG BOY'

The Union Pacific locomotive 'Big Boy' is believed to be the largest ever built. It is 40.5m long, and weighs over 350 tonnes. Its main wheels are taller than a man, and, at 2.74m, the diameter of its boiler is greater than the width of today's biggest lorry.

UNION PACIFIC LOCOMOTIVES

The biggest diesel locomotives were two which belonged to the Union Pacific Railroad in the USA. Each of them weighed over 426 tonnes. Working together, these two mighty machines could move a train that was nearly 5km long!

T.G.V.

The initials 'T.G.V.' stand for the French words 'Train à Grande Vitesse' . . . meaning 'very fast train'. This train holds the world rail speed record at over 515km/h. The electric locomotive that pulls the T.G.V. is not only the fastest in the world today, but, at 22.15m long, it is also the largest.

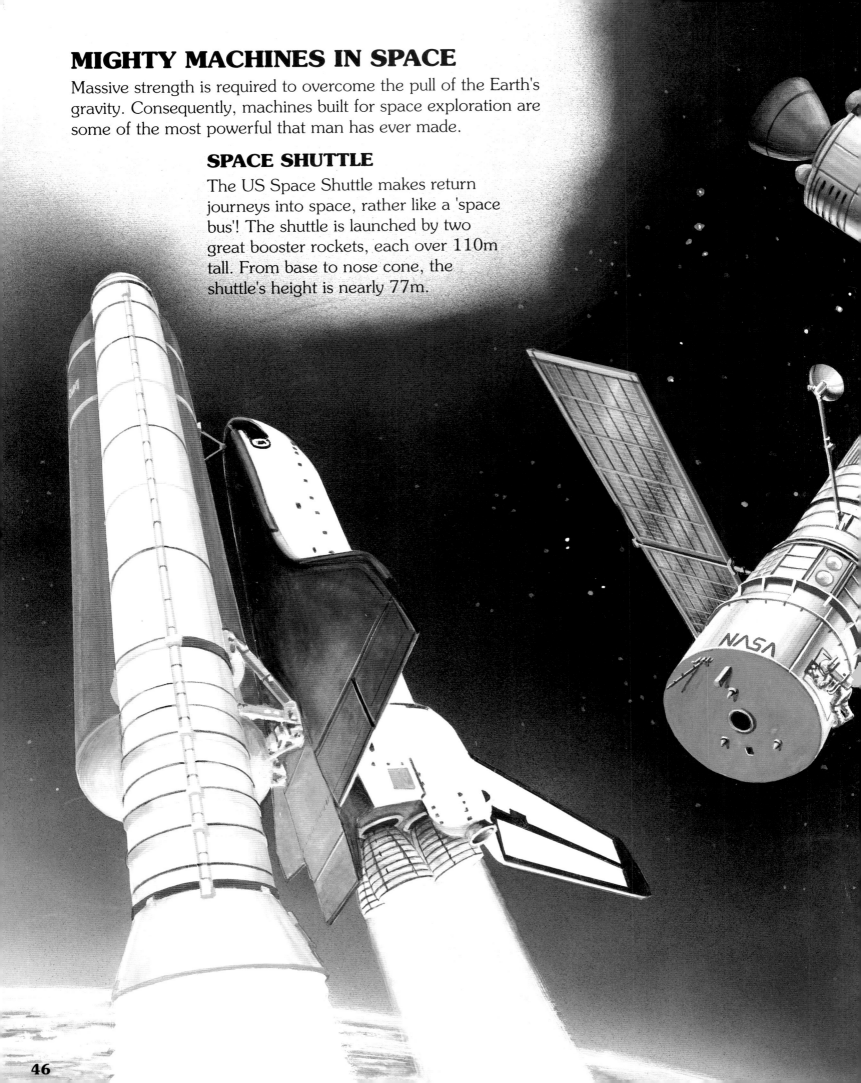

MIGHTY MACHINES IN SPACE

Massive strength is required to overcome the pull of the Earth's gravity. Consequently, machines built for space exploration are some of the most powerful that man has ever made.

SPACE SHUTTLE

The US Space Shuttle makes return journeys into space, rather like a 'space bus'! The shuttle is launched by two great booster rockets, each over 110m tall. From base to nose cone, the shuttle's height is nearly 77m.

HUBBLE SPACE TELESCOPE

This is a joint US-European space project, the first man-made satellite orbiting the Earth that is serviced by the space shuttle. The Hubble telescope can see stars which are 50 times *fainter* than those that can be viewed by the largest ground-based telescopes, and it can send back to Earth images from outer space. Powered by huge solar panels, the reflector of the telescope alone is 2.4m in diameter, and its over-all length is 4.26m.

SKYLAB SPACE STATION

This was the first US space station. It was launched into space in May, 1973, and was built within the empty third-stage fuel tank, nearly 54m long, of a Saturn V rocket. For 171 days it was operated as a space laboratory and observatory. One three-man crew spent 84 days on board. After the last crew completed their mission, Skylab was abandoned. It re-entered the atmosphere and broke up in July 1979.

Index